In the Beginning Was Love

In the Beginning Was Love

Psychoanalysis and Faith

by Julia Kristeva

translated by
Arthur Goldhammer

Columbia University Press
New York, 1987

Columbia University Press
New York   Guildford, Surrey
Copyright © 1987 Columbia University Press

Library of Congress Cataloging-in-Publication Data

Kristeva, Julia, 1941–
In the beginning was love.

(European perspective series)
Translation of: Au commencement était l'amour.
Includes index.
1. Psychoanalysis. 2. Psychoanalysis and philosophy.
I. Title. II. Series.
BF175.4.R44K7513   1987   150.19'5   87-24922
ISBN 0-231-06516-7

Clothbound editions of Columbia University Press are
Smyth-sewn and printed on permanent and durable
acid-free paper

Book design by J.S. Roberts

European Perspectives: A Series of Columbia University Press

Johan Goudsboom, *Sociology in the Balance* 1977
Norbert Elias, *What Is Sociology?* 1978
Raymond Boudon, *Crisis in Sociology* 1980
Arnold Gehlen, *Man In The Age Of Technology* 1980
Julia Kristeva, *Desire In Language* 1980
Franz Borkenau, *End And Beginning* 1981
Bero Rigauer, *Sport And Work* 1981
Marzio Barbagli, *Educating For Unemployment* 1982
Robert Castel, Francoise Castel and Anne Lovell,
    Psychiatric Society 1982
Gerard Genette, *Figures Of Literary Discourse* 1982
Niklas Luhmann, *Differentiation Of Society* 1982
Fernando Savater, *Childhood Regained* 1982
Eugenio Trias, *Artist And The City* 1982
Gilles Deleuze, *Nietzsche And Philosophy* 1983
Philippe Sollers, *Writing And The Experience
    Of Limits* 1983
Eugenio Trias, *Philosophy And Its Shadow* 1983
Francesco Alberoni, *Movement And Institution* 1984
Julia Kristeva, *Powers Of Horror* 1984
Julia Kristeva, *Revolution In Poetic Language* 1984
Richard Lowenthal, *Social Change
    And Cultural Crisis* 1984
Julia Kristeva, *Kristeva Reader* 1986
Daniel Roche, editor, *Journal Of My Life*:
    The Autobiography of Jean-Louis Menetra 1986

Contents

Foreword

Otto F. Kernberg, M.D.

This evocative, tersely written book combines an overt subject with an implicit, underlying theme. The overt subject is a contribution to the psychoanalytic understanding of the psychology of religious convictions—of faith. The underlying theme is a thoughtful French Lacanian analyst's critical, yet appreciative, disengagement from her theoretical background, as she makes her way on the road toward the contemporary mainstream of French psychoanalytic thinking.

Kristeva has in the past made significant contributions in the field of psycholinguistics. Here she presents a comprehensive statement of her approach to clinical psychoanalysis. In contrast to Lacan, she places affects rather than language at the center of the contents of the Unconscious, therein following another important French critic of Lacan—André Green—who also pointed to the weakness of Lacan's theory in neglecting the fundamental importance of affects. She retains Lacan's idea of the need for a dialectic relation between the imaginary and the symbolic in order to grasp the ultimately "real," namely, the existence of the dynamic Unconscious and its manifestations in the objective world of interpersonal discourse.

For the English-speaking psychoanalyst, Kristeva's language may be unfamiliar. Those not involved with Lacanian thinking will have to keep in mind that they are entering a psychoanalytic culture with a different language, as well as a different psychoanalytic perspective. Kristeva's firm clinical roots, however, her starting from and returning again and again to the clinical situation, provides psychoanalytic bridges for an understanding of and empathy with this viewpoint.

What is impressive in this book is the author's emphasis on the psychological structure of religion and its connection with psychopathology. Her dramatic and detailed presentation of a patient with a delusional system shows the relation between religion and hallucinatory wish-fulfillment. This same case serves as a background to illustrate her technique with psychotic regression as well as a basis for her understanding of religion. Kristeva's ideas in this area resonate with existential philosophy (which somehow evokes Heidegger's thinking—thinking that apparently originally also influenced Lacan).

In the past, psychoanalytic criticism of religion has been questioned on the basis of the assumption that the study of the unconscious roots of religious feelings, convictions, and aspirations does not invalidate the universal human search for a system of morality that transcends utilitarian needs and sectarian ideologies. To the contrary, it has been said that the assumption that psychoanalysis itself as a psychological science may provide the basis for such a system of universal values creates the danger of transforming psychoanalysis not only into an ideology but also into a religion. And when psychoanalysis becomes a religion it loses its scientific roots.

Kristeva, however, bypassing this dead-end street, proposes that a successfully completed psychoanalysis should help the individual free himself from protective illusions, the illusionary character of which he needed to deny in the past. At the same time, she expects that he will be able to open himself to the unavoidable urge to create and enjoy his own illusions, while recognizing their true nature. As she so eloquently puts it: "The more fortunate analysis and terminates with the renewed desire to question all received truths; as in the time of Heraclitus, he becomes capable once again of acting like a child, of playing."

This is a stimulating, rewarding book that may raise new questions for the English-speaking reader and, by the same token, also open a window to another "psychoanalytic scene." Kristeva joins the ranks of other distinguished contemporary French psychoanalysts such as François Roustang and Piera Aulagnier who, while distancing themselves from their Lacanian background, are bringing fresh observations and perspectives into psychoanalytic theory and practice.

Preface

When I was invited to express myself about "Psycho-analysis and Faith," I was at first quite reluctant. Juxtaposing the terms *faith* and *psychoanalysis* and the two realms of experience they designate seems to imply either that they can be reconciled or that they must remain implacable antagonists, when in fact the epistemological value and practical efficacy of psychoanalysis comes from its assertion of autonomy.

Yet isn't it the function of the analyst to pay heed to every question, not to answer them all, surely, but to displace, illuminate, or conjure away the object of interrogation? Every question, no matter how intellectual its content, reflects suffering. In our subject may lurk the suffering of religion as well as of rationalism, along with more strictly personal discomforts and anxieties. Let us try simply to be receptive to this suffering, and if possible to open our ears to meaning of another kind.

In the Beginning Was Love

Language and Subject
in Psychoanalysis

As *theology*, that once vast continent, vanished between the time of Descartes and the end of the nineteenth century, psychoanalysis (along with linguistics and sociology) became the last of the scientific disciplines to set itself up as a rational approach to the understanding of human behavior and its always enigmatic "meaning." Unlike the other human sciences, however, psychoanalysis has not been faithful to the positivist conception of rationality. Freud divorced psychoanalysis from psychiatry so that it might encompass a domain which for many is still that of the "irrational" or "supernatural." In fact, the object of psychoanalysis is simply the *linguistic exchange*—and the accidents that are a part of that exchange—between two subjects in a situation of *transference* and *countertransference*.

The technique and major assumptions underlying psychoanalytic treatment are today sufficiently widely known that it is not necessary to dwell on them at length. Such analytic concepts as the oedipus complex, libido, dream symbolism, and the death instinct are well known, if often denounced as rigid and simplistic. But these have little to do with the private and strictly individual practice of psychoanalysis, which cannot be discussed from outside. Psychoanalysis expresses itself either directly in the first person or else as depersonalization and loss; it is either rapture or pain.

Unfortunately, psychoanalysis has not been able to escape the attention of the mass media; it has become something of a fashion. The lectures on which this book is based might not otherwise have been commissioned. But this aspect of the subject is of little importance.

So far from being "victims" of these contemporary phenomena, analysts have wittingly or unwittingly taken part in them. Today it has even become fashionable to disparage psychoanalysis, just as it was fashionable a few years ago to accept its claim to be *the* new vision of the world, with solutions to every kind of crisis. But by relying on its observational techniques and testing its theories, psychoanalysis has maintained its relevance and ensured that it will be as effective tomorrow as it is today.

The practice of psychoanalysis is too complex to summarize, but let me remind you of several elements that I think go to the heart of the question. The analytic subject, or analysand, in substance says the following: "I am suffering from a primitive trauma, often sexual in nature, a deep narcissistic injury, which I relieve by displacing it onto the analyst. Here and now the omnipotent author of my being or malady (my father or mother) is the analyst. The deep meaning of my words is governed by this hidden drama, which presupposes that I grant considerable power to the analyst. But the confidence that I place in him is based on my love for him and what I assume is his love for me."

This mobilization of two people's minds and bodies by the sole agency of the words that pass between them sheds light on Freud's famous remark, in *The Future of an Illusion*, that the foundation of the cure is "Our God Logos." It also recalls the words of the Gospels: "In the beginning was the Word" (John 1:1) and "God is love" (1 John 4:8).

To be sure, analytic discourse does not, or at any rate does not always, suffer from the apparent excesses of amorous language, which range from hypnotic fascination with the presumed ideal qualities of the partner to hysterical sentimental effusion to phobias of abandonment. Nevertheless, it is want of love that sends the subject into analysis, which proceeds by first restoring confidence in, and capacity for, love through the transference, and then enabling the subject to distance himself or herself from the analyst. From being the subject of an amorous discourse during the years of my analysis (and, in the best of circumstances, beyond them), I discover my potential for psychic renewal, intellectual innovation, and even physical change. This kind of experience seems to be the specific contribution of our modern civilization to the hisory of amorous discourse. The analytic situation is the only place explicitly provided for in the social contract in which we are allowed to talk about the wounds we have suffered and to search for possible new identities and new ways of talking about ourselves. I assume, moreover, that it is my definition of the transferential discourse as a new kind of "love story"[1] that prompted the invitation to lecture on "psychoanalysis and faith."

Because analytic speech is a discourse of love it has qualities from which its efficacy derives; these same qualities reveal essential (but not very obvious) laws common to all speech acts. What are they?

The analytic setting is a paradoxical one: there is a couch on which one person lies down and speaks, and an armchair in which another person sits and listens; the motor faculties are thus blocked, and the displacement of instinctual energies into speech is facilitated. Insofar as that form of analytic discourse known as "free association" involves transferential, that is, amorous, language, it ceases to be merely intellectual and becomes, implicitly, emotional. Hence it cannot be understood in terms of a linguistic model that divides verbal signs into "signifier" and "signified." Analytic language works with signs that encompass representations of at least three types: representations of words (close to the linguistic signifier), representations of things (close to the linguistic signifed),[2] and representations of affects (labile psychic traces subject to the primary processes of displacement and condensation, which I have called *semiotic* as opposed to the *symbolic* representations inherent in, or derivative of, the system of language).[3]

To say that signification is *significance* embracing these three types of representations is not simply a way of

1. Julia Kristeva, *Histoires d'amour* (Paris: Denoel, 1983).

2. Sigmund Freud, *La Métapsychologie* (Paris: Gallimard, 1952).

3. See Julia Kristeva, *La Révolution du langage poétique* (Paris: Seuil, 1974), ch. I.

introducing dynamism into the notion of signification by adding an active suffix (-*ance*), nor is it intended to resurrect a medieval sense of the word. The point is to go beyond the theater of linguistic representations to make room for pre- or translinguistic modalities of psychic inscription, which we call semiotic in view of the root meaning of the Greek *semeion*: trace, mark, distinctive feature. At the very beginning of philosophy, before thought was constricted by the notion that language must reflect ideas, Plato, recalling the work of the atomists, spoke in the *Timaeus* of the *chora*, an ancient, mobile, unstable receptacle, prior to the One, to the father, and even to the syllable, metaphorically suggesting something nourishing and maternal.

My attempt to conceive a psychic modality logically and chronologically prior to the sign, to meaning, and to the subject may remind philosophers of this Platonic insight. I am of course following the lead of Freud, who sought to diversify the *types of representations* in psychic dynamics by including representations that can to one degree or another be subsumed in language but not grasped by the conscious mind. By specifying more fully than Freud does the status of those emotional traces that I call semiotic, I obtain a theoretical instrument for clarifying the *heterogeneous* nature of conscious and unconscious representations. Such an instrument is needed because one can observe in the clinic a psychic modality in which desire, anxiety, or narcissism leads to an eclipse of *signification* in the subject without thereby robbing his or her language of instinctual *meaning*, which records bioenergetic signals in the form of fluid but persistent psychic traces (as in narcissistic personality disorders and psychoses).

To be sure, the layering of significance that is an intrinsic part of analytic language also occurs in other kinds of discourse. But analytic transference accentuates it and makes it easier to observe. A stratified concept of significance enables us to understand how logical language, bolstered by infralinguistic (semiotic) representations, can find physical expression. We thus develop a powerful model of the human in which language is not divorced from the body; "word" and "flesh" can meet at any moment, for better or for worse.

From this tissue of meanings, ranging from prelinguistic emotional traces to linguistic representations and, by extension, to ideologies (symbolic representations), the analyst attempts to interpret the essential discourse of his patients, that is, their symptoms and fantasies.

Your headache, your paralysis, your hemorrhage may be the somatic return of an unsymbolized repressed object. The repressed language of hatred or love, or of emotions too subtle for words, then reactivate energies no longer filtered by any psychic trace or representation; these attack and disrupt the functioning of the body's organs. Mute signs are deflected into *symptoms*. Or perhaps you are obsessed by figments of your imagination, figures of your desire, stimulating enough to be exhausting, gloomy enough to be depressing. The analyst never looks upon symptoms and fantasies as aberrations but instead sees them as truths of the speaking subject, even if to cool judgment they seem to be delusions. I take them seriously, then, but as references to the past; by reviving them in therapy, I immolate them. They do not disappear, however, but at best assume a new configuration, one that we hope is more beneficial for the subject and those around him.

Etymologically analysis means dissolution: ανα from top to bottom, across; λύω pr., aor. ελύαα, f., λύσω to destroy, unbind, dissolve, pay; Latin, *luo*, to pay, expiate; *solvo*, to unbind, from *se-luo*; Sanskrit *lu-na-ti*, to cut, divide, annihilate; Gothic, *fra-liusan*, to lose; Latin, *luxus*, dislocated; etc.

Analysis strictly speaking exacts payment of the price set by the subject for revealing that his or her complaints, symptoms, or fantasies are discourses of love directed to an impossible other—always unsatisfactory, transitory, incapable of meeting my wants or desires. Yet by revealing to my analyst the wants and desires I feel, I give them access to the powers of speech and at the same time bring the powers of speech into ostensibly nameless recesses of meaning. Thus I gain access to my symptoms; I orchestrate my fantasies or I eliminate them, sometimes ably, sometimes less so.

My commitment to analysis (intermittent throughout, but no less intense than at the beginning), which through the person of the analyst carries me toward a focal point of power and knowledge—in a narcissistic fusion, an indispensable idealization given the weakness I experience as a premature and separate creature—is ultimately shaken by the discovery that the other is fleeing me, that I will never possess him or even touch him as my desires im agined him, ideally satisfying. What is more, this discovery reveals that I myself, at the deepest level of my wants and desires, am unsure, centerless, and divided. This does not eliminate my capacities for commitment and trust but makes them, literally and in no other way, *playable* (in the sense that a piece of music is playable).

Thus, undergoing psychoanalysis reveals the paradoxical nature of subjectivity. Let us assume that it is legitimate to speak of a "subject" as long as language creates the identity of a speaking agency and ascribes to that agency an interlocutor and a referent. The vast domain of the Freudian unconscious, with its representations of objects and semiotic traces of affects, remains subsidiary to language and becomes real only in a relation of desire, of speech for the other. Now, the "other scene" of the Freudian unconscious already discloses the essentially heterogeneous nature of the human being. At the extreme limit of the psychic traces, however, beyond the *representations* of words or things, we find the ultimate *marks* of the biochemical processes that take place in a subject interacting with another subject; hence these marks are already pre-signs, preconditions, or substrates of desire and communication.

As speaking beings, always potentially on the verge of speech, we have always been divided, separated from nature. This split has left within us traces of the pre- or translinguistic semiotic processes that are our only access to the species memory or the bioenergetic neuronal maps. These semiotic processes (archaic traces of the links between our erogenous zones and those of the other, stored as sonorous, visual, tactile, olfactory, or rhythmic traces) diachronically constitute a *presubject* (the *infans*). Synchronically they display the catastrophic anguish ("passion") of depressive psychosis. Their force scratches our on the whole fragile lucidity, causing our memory to lapse, our minds to whirl, our heads to fill with phantoms.

We are no doubt permanent subjects of a language that holds us in its power. But we are subjects *in process*, ceaselessly losing our identity, destabilized by fluctuations in our relations to the other, to whom we nevertheless remain bound by a kind of homeostasis. By postulating this *eclipse* of subjectivity at the dawn of our life, by sensing a *hiatus* in subjectivity in moments of intense passion, the psychoanalyst does not "biologize man's essence," as Heidegger feared. He places, instead, exorbitant confidence in the power of transference and interpretive language, knowing from experience that they are capable, once recognized and hence named eclipse and hiatus of the subject, of reestablishing the provisional unity of that subject and thus of preparing it for the further trials set by the life process of the passions.

Termination of the analysis signals the dissolution of certain fantasies as well as of the analyst, whose omnipotence is put to death. The depression that accompanies termination is a sign that this stage has come, which in the case of a successful analysis precedes the resumption of transitory, ludic illusions. Fantasy returns to our psychic life, but no longer as cause for complaint or source of dogma. Now it provides the energy for a kind of artifice, for the art of living.

The Unshakable Illusion

Freud saw religion as nothing less than an illusion, albeit a glorious one, like the misunderstandings of Christopher Columbus or the alchemists.[4] Like those prescientific beliefs from which modern geography and chemistry were born, religion for Freud is a rather unrealistic construct which nevertheless gives an accurate representation of the reality of its subjects' desires. In so doing it discovers psychic patterns, of which it is enough to change the name (a change of no small moment, however) to satisfy the criteria of scientific judgment. Freud is candid about one concern, however: might not "scientific reality" also prove to be an "illusion"? His answer is a firm no, even though his study of human desire had taught him that the future of illusion was assured.

Having observed how difficult it is for human beings to bear the collapse of their fantasies and the thwarting of their desires without succumbing to still other illusions whose unreality and irrationality they fail to perceive, Freud attempted to identify what secondary gain illusions might provide. In one chapter of *The Future of an Illusion* Freud tells of the letter sent him by an American

4. Sigmund Freud, *The Future of an Illusion* (New York: Norton, 1975).

doctor (who identifies himself as a "brother physician") critical of the psychoanalyst's atheism and recounting the story of his own conversion. Originally an atheist, this doctor claimed that he was struck by a glimpse of the "sweet face" of an old woman on an operating table. He thereupon rebelled against the divine injustice that had condemned so perfect a creature to suffer and die. There is of course something astonishing about such a reaction on the part of a grown man, and a physcian to boot, who must have seen far worse injustices. Then, suddenly, without explanation or mediation, the "brother physician" receives a revelation and accepts the truth of the Bible.

Freud's interpretation is as follows: the old woman's face reminded the doctor of his beloved mother. The first stage of the oedipal reaction is rejection of the father figure, readily associated with the arbitrary will of God. In the end, however, this impulse "succumbs to a powerful countercurrent. Over the course of the conflict the level of displacement is not maintained. No arguments are given to justify God, nor does the doctor say by what indubitable signs God proved his existence to him. Conflict seems to have taken the form of hallucinatory psychosis; inner voices persuaded the doctor to cease his resistance to God." This displacement of the oedipal conflict into a religious embrace of the Almighty can occur because religion has knowingly and subtly elaborated an account that makes room for and justifies the hallucination, that makes the hallucination plausible by granting the son, after his period of suffering, the glory that comes of identification with the father.

When hallucination encounters religion, the result is not always an attenuation of the hallucination to the level of socially acceptable fantasy. Yet even the paroxysm of hallucination can provide a temporary resolution. Less crushing a burden than the suffering due to burning desire or abandonment, hallucination can help the subject reestablish a kind of coherence, eccentric or aberrant though it may be. The resulting imaginary identity can sustain the individual and temporarily help him go on living.

Paul came to see me after an abortive first attempt at analysis following hospitalization at Sainte-Anne for, as he put it, "insanity." He is a man of sober appearance, precise in speech, intelligent, and capable of telling his story in a skillful and charming way that takes full advantage of dramatic silences and seductive turns. I am struck by the force of his rhetoric and the discreet strength of his personality, which effectively conceals underlying conflict, fragility, and confusion. Perhaps it was my sustained and sincere interest in the *meaning* of his narrative, which I did not hide, that persuaded Paul to abandon his skillful actor's facade and, in our first interview, tell me about what he called the "uncommon and almost incommunicable" drama of his life.

The youngest of three children, born after a sister and a brother, Paul was the son of a woman who had wanted another daughter; his first name was to have been Pauline. Tragedy struck when Paul was four (although as it turned out later, this tragedy camouflaged a very difficult early childhood for this young man of precocious intelligence beset by threats, emotional scenes, and phantoms). His father, a high official in the French colonial administration, was brutally tortured and murdered while his family watched. By itself an event such as this would be enough to destroy a life. But in this case it was linked to another event, the importance of which it heightened and dramatized. A year before, Paul had surprised his mother with a lover. The little boy had adored his mother, with whom he remembered having a relationship so close that it bordered on identification. (Wasn't he supposed to have been born a girl? And everyone said he was the spitting image of his mother.) This relationship between son and mother was almost cannibalistic: the son was avid for the mother's breast and body. The mother, upset at having been found out, made a violent scene in front of the boy: "If you say anything, I'll never speak to you again." Thus the first explicit murder of the father was committed by the son and his mother acting as accomplices. As a corollary to this, the mother threatened to withdraw her love if Paul chose a symbolic alliance with the father; she also forbade him to speak.

The conflict had to be kept hidden. Paul now became the prisoner of his mother, who had betrayed not only the father but also the son, and of their twin guilt (his oedipal act remained unspeakable, and her adultery was to be kept secret). Paul took refuge in solitude and spent long days in the woods—torturing snakes. With his father's murder his guilt reached its zenith: was he not an accomplice in his father's humiliation? Worse still, since the person humiliated was also himself, he saw himself tortured and killed in his father's place. From then on he behaved as though more dead than alive.

Shortly thereafter, while walking alone, Paul heard voices: "You will draw," they said, "you will become a painter of genius." These voices excited and frightened him. He never spoke of them to anyone. For a time, he says, he forgot about them, only to have them reappear when he was ten or twelve. They had been with him ever since. Thus his mother's commandment, "Thou shalt not speak," was superseded by a hallucinatory voice that said, "Thou shalt draw." In this way Mama would be happy (for Paul would not speak), yet Papa would have his loyal witness (Paul would draw pictures of a happy childhood or of his father's murder).

Paul excelled at drawing in school and later successfully took courses in technical drawing. During latency and governed by the obsessional code of apprenticeship, his hallucination found sufficient support that it could, without risk, take the form of intellectual activity sanctioned by the superego. At puberty, however, and subsequently during a prolonged adolescence, his violent desires reawakened. The voices still said, "Thou shalt draw." But now drawing and painting led to madness. The moment he immersed himself in painting, Paul lost control and began raving. Unable to speak to anyone, immured in boundless desires and hatreds, the colors of paint, chromatic signs, were of no use in containing anxiety due to incestuous appetites, murderous ambitions, or narcissistic worries (am I a boy or a girl?). Madness came as an attempt to arrange—as one might compose a painting—a fragment of language that may have had *meaning* for the subject (because it expressed his instincts and defenses) but lacked *signification* for anyone else, all others being obstinately pushed away. Hence the patient was hospitalized, given neuroleptics, and all the rest.

The transference, which proved feasible, encouraged Paul to talk for the first time about his voices: their "origin" in childhood, their reappearance, and their insistence. "You know you can't talk about such things, because in the first place nobody is interested, and in the second place it looks crazy." After making this confession and telling a number of subsequent stories, Paul told me that the voices had ceased. Did this mean his delusions were gone? Certainly not. In the transference, however, his delusion took the form of shifting the violence of his loves and hatreds onto me. Sometimes he forgets that I am only I and relives with me once-repressed feelings concerning his parents. But he is a long way from being reconciled. "You take part of me apart with your interpretations. You make me shift everything onto an intellectual level or something. But there are other parts of me. The central part is a great black mountain of granite, immense and immovable. And the two sides of me don't meet." (I think to myself of the traumatic scene in which Paul witnessed his mother's body touched by an unknown man, and of the other horrible scene in which he saw his father's body dismembered.) I tell him, at any rate, that he is right, that there is another part of him, but that I can *see* and *hear* that "untouchable mountain of granite": it may be a mountain of silent hatred seeking a way to express itself, or a mountain of betrayed love.

Our sessions are stormy: hyperintellectual at times, with discussions of aesthetics or metaphysics; other times tumultuous psychodramas in which the "granite mountain" produces emotional offspring in the form of fierce glances, cries, accusations that I am an evil, extraterrestrial power with laser eyes "that nail you to the ground and turn you into a zombie." Slowly words take the place of frozen terror and desire, sometimes easily, sometimes not. Still more primitively, words salve the wound of not having been desired for what he was, of having been stillborn, a dead Pauline rather than a living Paul. For his mother's deadly passion I was obliged to substitute, almost unwittingly, a vibrantly living investment in Paul's language, person, and life. Every pregnant woman fantasizes about the death of her baby, but some women, in order to protect their own narcissistic identities, may symbolically murder their offspring. Perhaps we need to invent a new term for them: the Lady Macbeth complex.

Together, then, we created a world, which to the objective observer (for objective observation is also part of my role as analyst) is completely unreal and illusory, an amalgam of pretenses, games, and masks. We are in a sense actors who take up our roles at the beginning of each session. But this imaginary relationship is able to accommodate the very real violence of Paul's memory, rendered mortal and lethal by repression. His was a memory that another person had wished to murder, yet it was able to survive, displaced and condensed, in drawing and painting. Finally, through the dramaturgy of psychoanalytic language, it was brought back to life. At one point in the therapy Paul brought me his drawings, which he had previously refused to show me: "They're explosive," he had said. I agreed to look at them, to let him try to develop the story they concealed by reconstructing his own invisible place in the picture, his rage, or, in rare instances, his happiness.

I want to stress the fact that the function of the psychoanalyst is to reawaken the imagination and to permit illusions to exist. The function, or one of the functions? There is no question that analytic treatment of psychoses, more common now than in Freud's day, requires that the resurrection of the imagination be given first priority in the treatment; the therapeutic role of the imaginary graft (greffe imaginaire) is thus magnified. If we look closely at the matter, however, it becomes clear that the structure of analytic language is essentially determined by a mnemonic technique, free association. Analytic discourse—in the first place that of the analysand, but also that of the analyst insofar as he listens to and attempts to deflect the discourse of the analysand through interpretation—issues from the web of imagination. It works with enticements, shams, approximations, "truths hic et nunc," to arrive at truths that become absolute only because they first find their exact meaning in the evanescence of the imaginary construct. By emphasizing only the verbal substance of the transference, without highlighting the fact that it involves not just playacting but, initially at least, mystification, we miss the imaginary aspect of psychotherapy. But it is precisely because analytic discourse is not definitively stabilized by verifiable argument and rational judgment that it is able, as a discourse of the imagination, to work on three levels at once (representations of words, representations of things, and semiotic traces of emotions), thereby obtaining the physical efficacy, the real impact that we desire.

By chastely neglecting this fundamental aspect of the analytic economy, psychoanalysis was able to appeal to science to validate its interpretations. Nevertheless, to say that an interpretation is uniquely correct and scientific ("this fantasy is nothing but a projective identification," "this symptom is nothing but an hysterical identification") depends on an evaluation, based to be sure on verifiable criteria but applied to an object that is fundamentally an object of the imagination: the amorous discourse of the analysand and the (more or less identificatory or projective) construct that the analyst derives from it. It cannot be overemphasized that analytic "truth" is woven out of a relationship, which makes it resemble not so much the discourse of faith as narrative fiction. In both religion and psychoanalysis a destabilized subject constantly searches for stabilization.

Far be it from me to belittle the scientific ambitions of psychoanalysis. In view of its modern technique (transferential discourse that reveals the underlying structure of what is said) and rigorous models (constantly tested in clinical practice and increasingly challenged by neurobiology), we can say that psychoanalysis is scientific discourse of a new kind. New because it does not abstract from or neutralize the subject of knowledge. On the contrary, the subject, through his very involvement in the listening process, constructs the object of psychoanalytic interpretation. That is the radical innovation on the basis of which analysis builds a model and a modification, a truth and a therapeutic, following the classic rules of scientific epistemology. Because my subject here is "psychoanalysis and faith," I cannot pursue this fundamental question of the scientific status of psychoanalysis any further. Let me simply stress that, because psychoanalysis is a different kind of science, we must be clear about the fact that its object is something that emerges from the imagination.

In sum, then, the effect of scientific truth—unique and verifiable—on the subject of an interpretation depends in part on the rigor of the underlying theoretical model and in part on the construction of a relationship or a language whose "historical reality" is of little importance; all that counts is the meaning, at first imaginary and therefore also real and symbolic, that is established between analysand and analyst. Whether or not you have actually experienced what you tell me is of little importance if through your illusion, your lie, or your madness I am able to grasp the impact (for me) and the logic (for all of us) of your symptoms and fantasies.

Paul did not walk out of our meetings neutral and calm merely because he had filled them with his fantasies. Our verbal confrontation proved, in fact, that his fantastic discourse—his stories and memories—had assumed more varied and perhaps more subtle forms. In this respect analysis, like illusion, seems interminable.

The analyst today is in a position different from that of Freud. He is less scrupulously a rationalist, or perhaps one should say less guilty in the face of rationalism and still less optimistic about the beneficial powers of reason. What today's analyst must do, I think, is restore to illusion its full therapeutic and epistemological value.

Does this mean restoring value to religion as well? Not altogether.

Credence-Credit

As *you know*, the history of patristics consists in large part of controversies over the definition of faith. There is discussion of the relative importance of rational certainty versus grace and of the relation among the Father, the Son, and the Holy Spirit. Heresy and dogma derive from these controversies, which I shall not explore here. For the sake of simplicity I shall consider the Credo, the basis of Catholic faith and cornerstone of the Church. But before reading this text, let us attempt a direct, naive phenomenology of faith.

I am not a believer, but I recall having been born into a family of believers who tried, without excessive enthusiasm perhaps, to transmit their faith to me. My unbelief was not, however, a matter of oedipal rebellion and signal of a rejection of family values. In adolescence, when Dostoevsky's characters first began to impress me with the violence of their tragic mysticism, I knelt before the icon of the Virgin that sat enthroned above my bed and attempted to gain access to a faith that my secular education did not so much combat as treat ironically or simply ignore. I tried to imagine myself in that enigmatic other world, full of gentle suffering and mysterious grace, revealed to me by Byzantine iconography. When nothing happened, I told myself that faith could not come until I had endured difficult trials. The road to belief was blocked, perhaps, by the lack of hardship in my life. But the vitality, not to say excitability, of my adolescent body came between mournful images of death and everyday reality, and my macabre thoughts soon gave way to erotic daydreams.

Later, in reading about famous mystical experiences, I felt that faith could be described, perhaps rather simplistically, as what can only be called a primary identification with a loving and protective agency. Overcoming the notion of irremediable separation, Western man, using "semiotic" rather than "symbolic" means, reestablishes a continuity or fusion with an Other that is no longer substantial and maternal but symbolic and paternal. Saint Augustine goes so far as to compare the Christian's faith in God with the infant's relation to its mother's breast. "What am I even at the best but an infant sucking the milk Thou givest, and feeding upon Thee, the food that perisheth not?"[5] What we have here is fusion with a breast that is, to be sure, succoring, nourishing, loving, and protective, but transposed from the mother's body to an invisible agency located in another world. This is quite a wrench from the dependency of early childhood, and it must be said that it is a compromise solution, since the benefits of the new relationship of dependency are entirely of an imaginary order, in the realm of signs. However intelligible or reasonable this dynamic may be (and theology excels at describing it), it appears to be driven, in es-

5. Saint Augustine, *Confessions*, E.B. Pusey, tr. (New York: Dutton, 1951), IV, I, I.

sence, by infra- or translinguistic psychic processes which behave like primary processes and gratify the individual in his or her narcissistic core. At the dawn of psychic experience Freud saw a primary identification, a "direct and immediate transference" of the nascent ego to the "father of individual prehistory," who, according to Freud, possessed the sexual characteristics and functions of both parents.[6]

This "direct and immediate transference" to a form, a structure, or an agency (rather than a person) helps to bring about primary stabilization of the subject through its enduring character; because it is a gift of the self, it both encourages and hinders the disintegrative and aggressive agitation of the instincts. This is perhaps what Christianity celebrates in divine love. God was the first to love you, God is love: these apothegms reassure the believer of God's permanent generosity and grace. He is given a gift of love without any immediate requirement of merit, although the question of just deserts does eventually arise in the form of a demand for asceticism and self-perfection. This fusion with God, which, to repeat myself, is more semiotic than symbolic, repairs the wounds of Narcissus, which are scarcely hidden by the triumphs and failures of our desires and enmities. Once our narcissistic needs are met, we can find images of our desires in stories recounting the experience of faith: the story of the virgin birth, for instance—that secret dream of every childhood; or that of the torment of the flesh on Golgotha, which mirrors in glory the essential melancholy of the man who

6. Sigmund Freud, *The Ego and the Id* (New York: Norton, 1963).

aspires to rejoin the body and name of a father from whom he has been irrevocably severed.

In order for faith to be possible, this "semiotic" leap toward the other, this primary identfication with the primitive parental poles close to the maternal container, must not be either repressed or displaced in the construction of a knowledge which, by understanding the mechanism of faith, would bury it. Repression can be atheist; atheism is repressive, whereas the experience of psychoanalysis can lead to renunciation of faith with clear understanding. The subsequent loss of a certain kind of pleasure brings the pleasure of another kind of understanding to the subject who has made such a decision; this other kind of understanding is not positive knowledge but strictly private, involving the fundamental dynamics of the psyche.

My adolescent rejection of faith probably had more to do with repression or with my overcoming auto-erotic guilt than with analytic detachment. By contrast, the ordeal of analysis requires, at a minimum, that I (analyst or analysand) accept the existence of an other. As Lacan rightly said, "There is an Other." The treatment of psychosis may suggest to the optimistic analyst that meaning—as well as the subject—is always already there, simply waiting to be established through his interpretation. A certain fideism, or even degraded forms of spiritualism, thereby find their way into psychoanalytic ideology. I hope, however, that through vigilant listening and strict adherence to interpretive logic we can be sure of continuing to see man as divided (both biological organism *and* talking subject, both unconscious *and* conscious), and to understand that man is (tenuously and intermittently) a subject only of the language enunciated by the other—the object, for each member of the group of his or her desires and hatreds. *Other* in language, otherness in speech, here and now rather than in some "other" world, the analyst listens and speaks, and by so doing makes the other less hellish ("Hell," said Sartre, "is other people"). The result is not to prepare that other for some sort of transcendental existence but rather to open up as yet undefined possibilities in this world.

Credo

"I *believe in* one God the Father Almighty. . . . "

    Credo: one of the most charged and enigmatic words in the European lexicon. Ernout and Meillet suggest the etymon **kred-oh* (see the Vedic *srad-dhati*, "he believes"), but the derivation leading to the Latin form *cred-* is not clear: the same with **dhe*, "to set down," which gives several Latin forms ending in *-do* (*condo*, "to set down together," *abdo*, "to locate far from," and *sacer dos*, **sakro-dho-ts*, "priest"). The composite **kred-dh* is formally impossible in Indoeuropean, where **kret-* and **dhe* were independent. The real problems have to do with **kret-*.

    Darmesteter was the first to interpret *credo*, *sraddhati*, **kred-dh-* as "to put one's heart into something." Ernout and Meillet feel that this "relation [with the heart] is a hypothesis for which there is no basis," and Benveniste makes a similar point when he remarks that in Indoeuropean "heart" can no more be a metaphor for life or spirit than "lung" or "kidney."[7] Mayrhofer, however, feels that the hypothesis is justified: *kred-*, he says, is the composite form of **kerd-*, whereas Ernout and Meillet assume an

---

7. Emile Benveniste, *Vocabulaire des institutions indo-européennes* (Paris: Editions de Minuit, 1969), 1:175.

alternating root, *k'erd-/krd*. Dumézil, who was at one time critical of Darmesteter's interpretation, has withdrawn his objections. According to the dictionary of Monier Williams, the corresponding Vedic word *srat-*, attested only in the composites *srad-dha-*, "to believe," and *srat-kar-*, "to vouch for, give assurance of," is considered in traditional Indian etymology a synonym of *satya-*, "truth." He sees a parallel between *srat-* and the Latin *cor, cordis*, as well as the Greek χαρδια.

Benveniste's comments on the question are important. After reviewing the various etymological interpretations, he argues that from the beginning *credo/sraddha* had both a *religious* meaning and an *economic* meaning: the word denotes an "act of confidence implying restitution," and "to pledge something on faith in the certainty that it will be returned," religiously and economically. Thus the correspondence between *credence* and *credit* is one of "the oldest in the Indoeuropean vocabulary." Vedic man deposits his *desire*, his "token," his "magical strength" (more than his heart) with the gods, trusting them and counting on their reward: *Indra* is the god of assistance, *Sraddha* the goddess of offerings. The Vedic religion, it has been said, can be summed up in the three terms faith, gift, and pleasure in giving. Having received the *srad*, god returns it to the believer in the form of his protection; trust in god is based on return, and "faith" implies certainty of remuneration. It is easy to see how the notion could have been secularized to mean "credit" in the financial sense. As for the heart, Christianity would later glorify it as the seat of faith. Saint Augustine was among the first to use this metaphor, for example, in his exhortation to "read the

Holy Scripture with your eyes fixed firmly on your heart."[8]

In its two-thousand-year history Christianity has known a variety of mystical experiences unique for their psychological subtlety: in extreme cases mystics have gone so far as to reject not only credit-recompense but even the very act of prayer, which they viewed as a selfish request. Nevertheless, in its general tenor and institutional embodiment the Christian faith appears not to be inconsistent with the Indoeuropean model of belief.

Do the Indoeuropean languages reflect a type of culture in which the individual suffers dramatically because of his separation from the cosmos and the other? Presumably implicit in such a separation and its attendant suffering is the act of offering—a bridge across the gap—together with the expectation of reward. The human, however, is immersed in the rhythms of the cosmos, which in the Indoeuropean world dominate the separation that underlies faith.

In reality, it is the biblical God who inaugurates separation at the beginning of creation. He creates a division which is also the mark of His presence: "In the beginning God created the heaven and the earth." *Bereschit*. The source and meaning of Christianity lie in Judaism, which Christians today seem to be rediscovering after years of separation. Psychologically, however, it is Christ's Passion, the "folly on the cross," as Saint Paul and Pascal called it, that reveals the somber division that is perhaps the

---

8. Saint Augustine, *De doctrina Christiana* IV, 5, 7.

paradoxical condition of faith: "Father, Father, why hast thou forsaken me?"

It is because I am separate, forsaken, alone vis-à-vis the other that I can psychologically cross the divide that is the condition of my existence and achieve not only ecstasy in completion (*complétude*: reunion with the father, himself a symbolic substitute for the mother) but also eternal life (resurrection) in the imagination. For the Christian believer the completion of faith is real completion, and Christ, with whom the believer is exhorted to identify, expiates in human form the sin of all mankind before achieving glory in resurrection. And yet we observe very real effects of imaginary identifications on the bodies and lives of our nonbelieving patients as well.

This pattern of faith may not be universal, however. The notion of a "gift of the heart" compensated by "divine reward" is apparently of relatively minor importance in Chinese religion, into which it was introduced by Buddhism. In classical Chinese (for example, the I *Ching*), "to believe" and "to be worthy of faith" are expressed by the word *xin*, where the ideogram contains the signs for *man* and *speech*. Does "to believe" therefore mean "to let speech act?" For Confucius *xin* is one of the cardinal virtues: one believes in a man who is worthy of confidence, in whose word one can trust. This moral, social, indeed commercial dimension of *xin* should not be allowed to obscure the fact that, fundamentally, the *xin* man is one who is in harmony with the *qi*, "the spirit" or "cosmic virtue." "If the sovereign is *xin*, he is the incarnation of cosmic virtue."

Thus the Confucians attach paramount value to truthful speech, whether individual, transindividual, or cosmic. Yet "there are fine but hollow words" and "Heaven says nothing" (Confucius). More radically, Lao Tse denounces words that are beautiful but false: "Credible speech is not beautiful, beautiful speech is not credible." He looks toward the transcendence of speech in something "beyond words," *wu yan*. This leaves the search for harmony with the *qi*. Not that man feels estranged from the cosmic spirit; rather, he is certain of being able to achieve a more complete harmony with it, in particular by various physical and linguistic means, such as calligraphy or *tai ji quan*. Contemplative "faith" as mere psychic experience is here supplanted by the possibility of permanent improvement by psychophysical means, sustained by the optimistic view that we are always part of the *qi*. If we could achieve this mode of being through comprehension alone, we could say that in Chinese tradition the separation of man from nature and of each man from the others is neither strictly localized nor strictly absolute. The *qi* derives from the *void*, which exerts its power as the "space between." But this "void" is not nothingness; in *qi xu*, the sign *xu*, which means "void," contains in stylized forms the ideograms for a "tiger" upon a "hill"; it evokes the breath of *yang* ready to pounce upon the *yin*.

Furthermore, in the Confucian triad heaven-man-earth, heaven and earth cannot fulfill their destiny without man. The Taoist equivalent for this triad is yang-"space between"-yin; thus in the dualities of Chinese religion

(Confucianism and Taoism) the parallel to man is the "space between."

Finally, in the spoken language "to believe" is *xin fu*, in which *fu* means "to wed," "to abandon oneself." This evocation of union between the two sexes and, more primitively, of a previous existence within the body of the mother is perhaps appropriate in a view of the world in which man is at one with nature and recommences creation with each of his actions. Here the psychic traces of physical and biological energies are accomodated, cultivated, polished, and harmonized with highly elaborate symbolic constructs; the only thing that seems to be lacking is the "metamorphosis of suffering." That, at least, is what a learned Chinese friend tells me—with regret, or ironic superiority?

Freud's pessimism notwithstanding, his discovery, inspired by and for the benefit of the suffering individual, may well effect that ludic metamorphosis that leads us, at the termination of treatment, to regard language as body and body as language. All plenitude turns out to be inscribed upon a "void" which is simply what remains when the overabundance of meaning, desire, violence, and anguish is drained by means of language. "A tiger leaps upon a mound." Approaching his patients with the aid of a model derived from his own analysis, the thearpist is able to apprehend psychic structures unknown to psychiatric nosography. He gives meaning to the "emptiness" of the "borderline" while teaching the patient to cope with the emptiness within self-understanding that is the original source of our anguish and moral pain.

Is psychoanalysis perhaps *also* our "China within?"

Credo in Unum Deum

An early Credo, known as the "Symbol" of the Apostles," was in use throughout western Christendom by the tenth century. The Credo quoted here, based on the Nicene Creed of 325, was worked out by the Council of Constantinople in 381 and has remained in use to the present day.

We believe in one God the Father Almighty, creator of heaven
    and earth, and of all things visible and invisible:
And in one Lord Jesus Christ, the only begotten Son of God, begotten
    of his Father before all worlds, God of God, Light of Light, very
    God of very God, begotten not made, being of one substance
    with the Father, by whom all things were made; who for us
    men and for our salvation came down from heaven, and was
    incarnate by the Holy Spirit of the Virgin Mary, and was made
    man, and was crucified also for us under Pontius Pilate. He
    suffered and was buried, and the third day he rose again ac-
    cording to the scriptures, and ascended into heaven, and sit-
    teth on the right hand of the Father. And he shall come again
    to judge both the living and the dead: whose kingdom shall
    have no end.
And we believe in the Holy Spirit, the Lord and giver of life,
    who proceedeth from the Father and with the Father and the

Son together is worshiped and glorified, who spake by the prophets. And we believe in one catholic and apostolic Church. We acknowledge one baptism for the remission of sins. And we look for the resurrections of the dead and the life of the world to come.

Whoever is speaking in this text does not define his faith except in terms of its object. The God to whom he entrusts his vital speech—his heart—is a trinity. He is first of all the "Father Almighty," the "creator" not only of the person praying but of "all things visible and invisible."

As if to bring himself closer to the person invoking his name, however, this God is also "Lord Jesus Christ, the only begotten Son of God." Begotten by God, he shares his essence, he is "one substance" with the Father; this is amplified by the statement that he is "begotten not made," since no creature can be identical with the Creator. This Son, with whom the person praying is supposed to find it easier to identify, is thus also a "son" (with a small *s*), a "minor" in some sense, yet still a "very God of very God," "Light of Light." Next we have various Christological assertions setting forth the history of the Son's time on earth. We are told that he came down from heaven for our salvation, that he made himself a man, becoming flesh by way of virgin birth from the body of a woman, the Virgin Mary. Like the person who invokes his name, this man suffered; he was crucified at a specific moment in history (under Pontius Pilate), he was buried, and on the third day (according to the sacred texts) he was restored to life and ascended to heaven and a place of glory at this

Father's side. Ultimately he will return on Judgment Day to judge the living and the dead.

Following this christological excursus we return to the exposition of the trinity. The Holy Spirit is worshiped and glorified jointly with the Son and the Father in whom it "originates." (The Eastern and Western Churches differed on this question, the former denying that the Holy Spirit originates with both the Father *and* the Son.) Like the other two persons of the trinity, the Holy Ghost was mentioned by the prophets. It gives life and serves as mediator: it is "through the Holy Spirit" that the Son was incarnated in the Virgin Mary.

The Credo ends by mentioning the institution that sustains the faith and to which we must also give our hearts. The "catholic and apostolic" Church is the locus of ritual and faith: baptism, confession, remission of sins. Thus from the trinitarian nexus to its "political apparatus" the believer is provided with a structure of support with the help of which he will be able to obtain a reward that no human gift can possibly equal: resurrection and eternal life in the centuries to come.

Does anyone in the West *believe* in all the elements of this admirably logical and unified system? If believers do exist, aren't they a bit like my analysand, many-faceted characters, prepared to accept the Credo in one of their parts or "personalities" while allowing others—the professional personality, the social personality, the erotic personality—to ignore it? Essential as this feature of contemporary religious belief is, it is not the question I wish to discuss here.

As an analyst, I find that the Credo embodies

basic fantasies that I encounter every day in the psychic lives of my patients. The almighty father? Patients miss one, want one, or suffer from one. Consubstantiality with the father and symbolic identification with his name? Patients aspire to nothing else, and the process is at once essential to psychic maturation and a source of pleasure (through assumption of the father's power and elevation to the summit of authority). More than any other religion, Christianity has unraveled the symbolic *and* physical importance of the paternal function in human life. Identification with this third party separates the child from its jubilant but destructive physical relationship with its mother and subjects it to another dimension, that of symbolization, where, beyond frustration and absence, language unfolds. Because of its insistence on the paternal function, Christianity shapes the preconscious formulation of the basic fantasies characteristic of male desire.

Thus the substantial, physical, incestuous fusion of men with their fathers both reveals and sublimates homosexuality. The crucifixion of God-made-man reveals to the analyst, always attentive to murderous desires with regard to the father, that the representation of Christ's Passion signifies a guilt that is visited upon on the son, who is himself put to death.

Freud interprets this expiation as an avowal of the oedipal murder that every human being unconsciously desires. But Christ's Passion brings into play even more primitive layers of the psyche; it thus reveals a fundamental depression (a narcissistic wound or reversed hatred) that conditions access to human language. The sadness of young children just prior to their acquisition of language has often been observed; this is when they must renounce forever the maternal paradise in which every demand is immediately gratified. The child must abandon its mother and be abandoned by her in order to be accepted by the father and begin talking. If it is true that language begins in mourning inherent in the evolution of subjectivity, the abandonment by the father—the symbolic "other"—triggers a melancholy anguish that can grow to suicidal proportions. "I detest him, but I am he, therefore I must die." Beyond the torment of suicide there is joy, ineffable happiness at finally rejoining the abandoned object.

The "scandal of the cross," the *logos tou stavron* or language of the cross, which some, according to Saint Paul, would call "foolishness" (I Cor. 1:18 and 1:23; Gal. 5:11) and which is indeed inconceivable for a god as the ancients understood the term, is embodied, I think not only in the psychic and physical suffering that irrigates our lives (*qui irrigue notre existence*) but even more profoundly in the essential alienation that conditions our access to language, in the mourning that accompanies the dawn of psychic life. By the quirks of biology and family life we are all of us melancholy mourners, witnesses to the death that marks our psychic inception.

Christ abandoned, Christ in hell, is of course the sign that God shares the condition of the sinner. But He also tells the story of that necessary melancholy beyond which we humans may just possibly discover the other, now in the form of symbolic interlocutor rather than nutritive breast. In this respect, too, Christianity wins the adhesion of the masses; it supplies images for even the fissures in our secret and fundamental logic. How can we not believe?

A virgin mother? We want our mothers to be virgins, so that we can love them better or allow ourselves to be loved by them without fear of a rival. The unprecedented affirmation of symbolic paternity (carried to the point of insisting on the consubstantiality of father and son) could not have been made without reducing the weight of certain images, which would have made the burden of the father's symbolic authority too heavy to bear; those images have to do with procreative sexuality. By eliminating the mother as well as the father from the primal scene, the believer's imagination protects itself against a fantasy that is too much for any child to bear: that of being supernumerary, excluded from the act of pleasure that is the origin of its existence. Christianity, it must be said, avoids the whole question of procreation and is thus profoundly influenced by the idea of the virgin mother, which Catholicism, particularly in its more exuberant baroque forms, carried to an extreme.

More than one mother has been sustained in narcissistic equilibrium by the fantasy of having a child without the aid of a father; such women are not necessarily paranoid. Yet female hysterics, frequently touched by paranoia as well, relish the not-so-humble role of the virgin mother who is the "daughter of her son," mother of God, queen of the Church, and to top it all off the only human being who does not have to die (even her son must endure the cross). For her life ends according to Orthodox dogma in "dormition" and according to Catholic dogma in "assumption." Such a view of maternity has a strong appeal to man's imagination, as we have seen; it is particularly stimulating to artistic sublimation, as the example of Leonardo proves.[9]

Unfortunately, the proscription of female sexuality helped to infantilize half the human race by hampering its sexual and intellectual expression. Only advances in contraceptive technique have finally made it possible to lift that proscription. Previously, however, women received generous compensation in the form of praise of motherhood and its narcissistic rewards. Hence today, now that so-called artificial pregnancies have given concrete reality to the distinction between sexuality and procreation, femininity and maternity, the image of the virgin mother resonates with the daydreams of modern women with no particular religious vocation simply because there is no secular discourse on the psychology of motherhood.

The Trinity itself, that crown jewel of theological sophistication, evokes, beyond its specific content and by virtue of the very logic of its articulation, the intricate intertwining of the three aspects of psychic life: the symbolic, the imaginary, and the real.

To the analyst, however, the representations on which the Credo is based are fantasies, which reveal fundamental desires or traumas but not dogmas. Analysis subjects these fantasies to X-ray examination. It begins by individualizing: What about *your* father? Was he "al-

---

9. Sigmund Freud, *Leonardo daVinci and a Memory of His Childhood*, Alan Tyson, trans. (New York: Norton, 1964).

mighty" or not? What kind of son were *you*? What about *your* desire for virginity or resurrection? By shifting attention from the "macrofantasy" to the "microfantasy" analysis reveals the underlying sexuality, which prayer circumvents but does not really proscribe; for though the object of desire be transformed, desire itself remains a feature of Christian discourse.

What is the role and significance of the sexualization of psychic life for which psychoanalysis is credited by some and blamed by others?

Sexualization

Spurred on by transferential love, the analysand begins to speak of his desires. Analytic interpretation then reveals the erotic underpinnings of his relations with other people.

The analytic experience in fact dredges up the libido buried under seemingly humble or pure desires and aspirations. Encompassing the death instinct as well, repressed sexuality turns out to be the point of interchange between, on the one hand, biological energy and its neurological traces (what scientists call the "neuronal map") and, on the other hand, psychic inscriptions and representations. The reproductive system is the essential link between the living individual and the species; this, together with the fact that the erogenous zones are especially sensitive, particularly in human beings, probably accounts for the central role of the sexual function in psychic life and for its function as intermediary between the neuronal map and meaningful representation. One day science may well discover some biochemical peculiarity of sexual excitement and its neuronal transmission that could account for the exact role of sexuality in the subject's psychic map. In the current state of research, however, this is impossible. Yet the key role that sexuality plays in relations with others and in ensuring the survival of the species establishes its fundamental importance in the structure of living things viewed as "open systems," that is, in interaction with the ecosystem and other individuals of the same species.

Furthermore, man's unique symbolic capacities (human language being the only known code of communication that is "doubly articulated": signifier/signified) both extend and augment his singularity among "open systems." Whatever phylogenetic relations there may have been between the sexual function and the development of language, it is clear that the two are closely dependent on one another; symbolism has a powerful influence on sexuality, which is consequently overdetermined in human subjects. If it is true that the progress of civilization was achieved through control of sexuality by means of symbolism, then that control must be relaxed in order to alleviate anxieties born of repression. The first and most "popular" effect of psychoanalysis was to challenge the perverse ways in which sexuality had been misused, whether religious, rationalistic, moralistic, or associated with the superego. Analysis proved that sexuality could not be understood by separating sex from language, for the two are related by an ineluctable dialectic. It sought to discover modes of meaning adequate for the most obscure or ineffable forms of sexual response. As Freud pointed out, art preceded psychoanalysis in exploring this terrain.

Sexuality, then, is a complex pattern of responses and meanings in the relations between one open system and another, one articulate subject and another. Hence it is more than what is called "erotic" in pulp novels and pornographic magazines. Analysts not only speak of infantile sexuality but, even more paradoxically, they look for traces of the libido even in narcissism, where the erotic appeal of the "other" is nil. Preverbal or transverbal manifestations of organic stimuli or functional impairments are seen as variants, dissimulated perhaps but not obscure, of a sexuality that is always meaningful and always seeking a name. Even the death instinct is a manifestation of sexuality when it subtends aggressive desires, desires to inflict pain on another person or on oneself (even to the point of death). Extinction of the libido (in the sense of meaningful desire for an object) is conceivable only in situations in which there is total divestment of all ties to other people and even to one's own narcissistic identity. Even then psychic structure is organized in terms of the significant responses of an articulate subject, however limited those responses may be.

Are we not abusing terminology when we expand the meaning of sexuality in this way? In the face of criticism by Jung, Freud stubbornly defended the practice on both epistemological and ethical grounds. Epistemologically, because if the preoedipal narcissism whose dramas dominate psychotic symptomatology (as opposed to neurotic symptomatology, in which oedipal issues dominate) is not stirred by erotic desire for an external object, it is nevertheless governed by the primitive biological and semiotic preconditions of such desire, which are ultimately determined by the erotic behavior of parents and other familiar adults. Ethically, because one of the functions of psychoanalysis (however limited) is to improve the patient's ability to articulate his pattern of response, to enable him to control and process (*métabolise*) his sexual feelings. Hence the sexualization of analytic and interpretive discourse, the articulation of desires (and in particular, at different stages of the transference, of desires for the analyst or the analysand), is the key test of the subject's unification *and* destabilization, a test that therapy must confront if it wishes to be something more than a sophisticated papering over of the patient's problems. Proof of the truth of an analysis requires at a minimum that it pass this test.

Last but not least, psychoanalysis is neither a manifesto for sexual liberation nor a method of enforcing some sort of "normal" sexuality. The psychoanalyst knows that human sexuality (as defined above) is by its very nature diverse. It is a central part of the human being viewed as an open system, and when it goes wrong, suffering is the result, suffering to which psychoanalysis responds. In doing so psychoanalysis reveals the intrinsic perversity of human sexuality. "Perverse" is no doubt too pejorative a word to apply with a clear conscience to the commoner forms of human sexuality. Yet it is accurate: we are narcissistic, incestuous, masochistic, sadistic, patricidal, and naturally attracted to or repelled by physical and moral types different from our own, hence aggressive toward others. But we can "make do" with human nature as it is. In any event we have no other choice. A word of love is often a more effective, profound, and durable treatment than electroshock therapy or psychotropic drugs; sometimes it is the only treatment for a condition that is no doubt a consequence not only of our biological nature but also, and *at the same time*, of an inopportune or ill-intentioned word.

Who Is Unanalyzable?

In transference the analyst risks the dissolution of his own knowledge, that is, of what the patient presumes his knowledge to be and of the knowledge that he has brought to bear in other cases. Each analysis modifies—or should modify—at least some of the beliefs about psychodynamics that I held before hearing what the analysand had to say. When treatment is complete, the function of the analyst is eliminated by the dissolution of the transferential bond. Does analysis favor a Stoic world composed of lonely men and women without ties to one another and without religion? Not really. Toward the end of therapy there is a moment of paranoia: "I am alone, hence I am the creator." Tragically, some analysands get no further than this. But the real end of analysis, if indeed the process ever ends, is more likely that which comes after the period of disillusionment, when a certain playfulness of spirit returns: "I am someone else, I cannot say who. There are things that cannot be said, and I am entitled to play around with them so that I can understand them better." Perversion is thus tamed, if you will. I am indeed alone, like no other person. Knowing this, I can also play for real, for keeps, at forming bonds: creating communities, helping others, loving, losing. Gravity becomes frivolity that retains its memory of suffering and continues its search for truth in the joy of perpetually making a new beginning.

I do not agree with Lacan that Catholics are unanalyzable. With a Credo like the one cited earlier, they have already begun the analytic process. Is it not true that analysis begins with something comparable to faith, namely, transferential love? "I trust you, and I expect something in return." Analysis ends, however, with the realization that I cannot expect anything in return unless I am willing to give myself to my benefactor, that demands and even desires make the subject the slave of its object. Once analyzed, I continue to make demands and to feel desires, but in full awareness of cause and effect. Knowledge of my desires is at once my freedom and my safety net. Now I can love and delude myself at my own risk. In this sense analysis is not less than religion but more—more, especially, than Christianity, which hews so closely to its fundamental fantasies.

Are Catholics unanalyzable? It is true that they put up a formidable resistance. Protestants *count with* the analyst; they cooperate with their heads more than with their sexuality. Jews *count on* the analyst: they give themselves and attempt to dominate. Catholics *count* only *for themselves*: hostile to the transference, more narcissistic or perverse than other patients, they are relative newcomers to analysis who pose new problems for the analyst as well as new avenues of research. "*Keep on counting*," say Muslims as they get up from the couch. "*Thank you for allowing yourself to be counted (accounted),"* is the polite formula employed by Japanese Shintoists, who avoid the crisis of transference. Still, the analyst, like Dante in hell, hears them all, as long as he brings passion and suffering to the encounter. He has only to adjust his ear to different cultures and traditions.

Children and Adults

Credence-credit. The linking of these two ideas may derive from primitive times, when a mankind still in childhood, separated from the mother, was forced to rely on the Other in order to survive. That Other may be the father, the king, the prince, the parliament, the party, the welfare state, or the intellectual. As long as we remain children (and who has completely escaped from childhood?), we need transference—a synonym for love and faith.

Another aspect of human existence is now seeking to express itself through psychoanalysis, however. I am thinking of humanity as it suffers from a "crisis of values," a humanity that no doubt remains a child, but a child that feels itself to be an orphan. For that humanity, the Other is in Me: I am an Other. This humanity lives in, and on, separation. Analysis is apprenticeship in separation as both *alienation* and *loss*. Analytic experience reveals that the discourse of the father, king, prince, or intellectual is *your discourse*. It is a logic that is within you, which you can domesticate but never dominate. Analytic discourse speaks of a humanity that is willing to lose in order to know itself as pure loss and thus pay its debts to the

Almighty; it aims for tenuous, temporary ties and relationships.

Analysis is a means of transition from trust to separation. I give my heart, then I reclaim it in order to risk it once more, ad infinitum. I am always prepared to be pushed off center without tragedy and with sufficient pleasure that I am ready afterward to renew relations with others.

Having discovered the essence of the other, I am able to settle in myself. "To settle in oneself" through love of the "essential good" is one of the aims of Thomist theology and ethics. Analysis gives me confidence that I can express all the parts of my being, and this confidence quells my narcissism and enables me to transfer my desire to others. I can then open myself up to the variety of experience that becomes possible with others who may be different from me or similar to me. What is more, the discovery of an other in me does not make me schizophrenic but enables me to confront the risk of psychosis, which is perhaps the only truly frightening hell.

Who are we? Grownups who attempt to rely on our own strengths, made available by the ability of language to reach even the most inaccessible traces of instinct and the most troubling representations of desire. For nearly a century now, psychoanalysis has sought to make itself our discourse. It is not hard to understand why psychoanalysis has flourished primarily in the Judeo-Christian West, with its advanced science and technology and its highly developed individual consciousness, rather than in the totalitarian countries of the Third World. What about the future, as we grapple also with the future of—tenacious—illusions?

Analysis reveals the frequently unpleasant truth about the libidinal economy and psychic interests on which we have built structures of love, work, and marriage. Are we prepared to accept this truth? Are we capable of altering it? The recent period, full of economic and political uncertainty and devoid of ideologcal conviction, would seem unlikely to foster the necessary courage. Yet this toppling of all the idols has actually cleared the way for analysis as the most radical approach to lucidity, with the speaking subject now installed at the center of the linguistic apparatus itself. I think: "Who am I?" And even: "Am I?"

But how many of us are capable of this? To reiterate, there is a shadow of Stoicism in the ethics of termination; whoever makes it through analysis gives proof of great powers of moral endurance, for he or she has looked unblinkingly at demystified images of self and community. Yet if analysis is more than just therapy but also a certain kind of ethic, then it has nothing in common with lay religion or the initiation rites of a sage. The analysand delves beyond childhood to discover the immemorial origins of his desires; in the course of his analysis he recreates his sense of time, alters his psychic economy, and increases his capacity for working-through and sublimation, for understanding and play. Cynicism may then become the tell-tale sign that a person has chosen social integration as the surest means of terminating his analysis. The more fortunate analysand terminates with a renewed desire to question all received truths; as in the time of Heraclitus, he becomes capable once again of acting like a child, of playing. As Spinoza showed, joy is the ultimate degree, beyond knowledge, which I shed in order to glimpse its source, in others, in the other. But is joy illusion or disillusion?

Our debate has necessarily emphasized certain of the more public, more ideological aspects of the analytic experience. In its current stage, however, psychoanalysis has more characteristically withdrawn from the public limelight, into which it had been forced by certain peculiarities of the history of the analytic movement in France. It has done so in order to deepen its understanding of new psychic structures and situations through the practice of psychotherapy, and to allow analytic technique to adjust to the sufferings and desires of modern individuals.

The "lay" issues that I have discussed here (concerning the technical aspects of psychoanalysis as science) will necessarily leave the researcher or clinician feeling rather frustrated. He will recognize, however, in a highly sublimated, socialized form, the primary issues of current analytic research: narcissism, depression, perversion, psychosomatic ills, and the role of sublimation in the face of anxiety (resistance or stimulus to working-through?).

I hope that my discussion of "psychoanalysis and faith" will have reformulated the problem in such a way as to touch the anxieties and philosophical or metaphysical concerns of my more religious readers.

Is Psychoanalysis
a Form of Nihilism?

If *you have* followed this deliberately unorthodox presentation this far, you have probably asked yourself if psychoanalysis is a form of nihilism. (The question is intrinsic to metaphysics and no doubt touches upon other concerns as well.)

When Nietzsche proclaimed at the end of the last century that "God is dead" (in his *Gay Science*), he was not echoing the cry of unbelievers who posit nothing (*nihil*) in the place of God. As Heidegger has shown, Nietzsche was confirming the "essential decline of the suprasensible," of the Ideal as "suprasensible world with the power to oblige and gratify."[10] This decline, of which Christianity itself might be considered one consequence (and therefore a form of nihilism), became particularly pronounced after Descartes and Leibniz. Those two thinkers reversed the status of Being, which became an object of subjective thought; every existent assumed the status of an object in the immanence of subjectivity. The "will to power" can thus be viewed as a craving for values based upon the

10. Martin Heidegger, "Le mot de Nietzsche 'Dieu est mort,'" in *Chemins qui ne mènent nulle part* (Paris: Gallimard, 1962).

59

assumption that absolute Value has collapsed, coupled with a desire to understand, to calculate, to compute. But Nietzsche hoped for a transvaluation of values which would infuse a new spirit into the life of the "superman." In a sense it is not incorrect to argue that Freud represents the culmination of the nihilist program.

For psychanalysis does indeed subvert the subject's being by viewing it as a psychic "object." Freud's view of the psyche encompasses even the "reasons of the heart" which were so mysterious to Pascal, yet calculation is implicit in the Freudian notion of a logic of the unconscious. Psychoanalytic theory, viewed as a theory of knowledge of psychic objects (consciousness, the unconscious, instinct, desire, etc.), is part of the nihilist effort to objectify man's being.

Nevertheless, analytic language (that spoken by the analysand as well as that spoken by the analyst insofar as the analyst himself remains an analysand) cannot be reduced to objective terms. The analytic process is first and foremost an unfolding of language, prior to and beyond all unification, distantiation, and objectification. Language thus resonates between two subjects, posed or de-posed. It opens or closes their bodies to its implicit ideals and offers a possiblity (not without risks) of psychic as well as physical life. Therapy as deployment of language in all its complexity, variety, and functionality integrates concern("Is not my desire for the other also a desire for death?") with the Ideal ("What am I without this web of desire in which I am trapped?"). Its vital efficacy is inseparable from its ethical dimension, which is commensurate with love: the speaking being opens up to and reposes in the other.

Because of the role ascribed to language, psychoanalysis stands in a new relation not only to the physical but also to the Ideal. After a lengthy process of remembering and self-discovery, the analysand learns to know himself, submrged though he is in the immanence of a significance that transcends him. That significance can be given a name: the *unconscious*. The analysand knows the unconscious, orders it, calculates with it, yet he also loses himself in it, plays with, takes pleasure from it, lives it. Psychoanalysis is both objectification and immersion; it is both knowing and, through language, unfolding. It is an extraordinary effort to recast our whole intellectual tradition from its inception to its annihilation. On the one hand there is nothing (*nihil*) but the knowing subject; on the other hand I know that that subject derives from an alien significance that transcends and overwhelms it, that empties it of meaning.

If psychoanalytic nihilism exists, it is a nihilism that encompasses both the subjectification *and* the objectification of man's being as a creature of language viewed in terms of his relations to others: openness, consolidation, increase. Through these relations, the analysand sheds his old self, yet without becoming a superman. Once he has recognized his desire he acquires a new desire for (self-) knowledge; the "new" man recognizes that he is caught in the toils of an unconscious logic, even though he can grasp the nature of that logic on a conscious level. Besides calculating knowledge we have a discourse that encompasses both allusion and illusion—displacements born of the interminable quest for an adequate fit between "meaning" and "object." This is the realm of imagination, play, and possibility, where even calculation becomes renewal and creation. At the very heart of our rationality, psychoanalysis refuses to be confined within the narrow bounds of rationalism. Inwardly it veers toward metaphysics (in the dual sense of separate Ideality and potential Objectification), yielding not only maximal lucidity but also a sacrifice of lucidity for which one need not feel any guilt. Has desire, the ultimate sign of subjectivity, therefore triumphed? The self has also subordinated itself to the other for the sake of a necessary, if temporary, tie.

As one hears all too often nowadays, life in the midst of modern technology has itself become an object, a product of the work of chemists, surgeons, and genetic engineers serving power-hungry men and women. As the "rights of man" are expanded to embrace Godlike powers, the analyst detects the manic cry of the nihilist: "The Creator is dead, and I have taken his place." Psychoanalysis, bridging the gap between the two aspects of metaphysics mentioned above, offers not only a language but also a way of life in fragile equilibrium between hedonism and concern for transcendent meaning, which can annihilate the self but also lead the self to annihilate others. The humanist's respect for the other stems from his ability to renounce the will to dominate. Seen in psychoanalytic terms, the rights of man comprise not the right to calculate what life is but to *understand the unconscious*, to understand it even to the gates of death. Psychoanalysis thus sheds a sardonic light on the individual will to dominate existence, and life as the ultimate value of existence. It is the height of nihilism to claim, in the name of the rights of man—or superman—rights over life itself. The analyst takes another view: he looks forward to the ultimate dissolution of desire (whose spring lies in death), to be replaced by relationship with another, from which meaning derives.

No restrictive, prohibitive, or punitive legislation can possibly restrain my desire for objects, values, life, or death. Only the meaning that my desire may have for an other and hence for me can control its expansion, hence serve as the unique, if tenuous, basis of a morality. In my opinion, therefore, psychoanalysis is the modest if tenacious antidote to nihilism in its most courageously and insolently scientific and vitalist forms. It is the superman's shield and protection. For how long?

DATE DUE

JUN 01 '90			
FEB 2 4 2003			
APR 0 2 2019			